LIVING THINGS

By · ADRIENNE · MASON

PHOTOGRAPHS BY RAY BOUDREAU

Heinemann

*Heinemann Children's Reference and Kids Can Press Ltd acknowledge
with appreciation the assistance of the Canada Council, the Ontario Arts
Council and Gavin Barrett in the production of this book.*

First published in Canada in 1997 by Kids Can Press Ltd,
29 Birch Avenue, Toronto, Ontario, Canada, M4V 1E2.
This edition published in Great Britain in 1997 by
Heinemann Children's Reference, an imprint of Heinemann
Educational Publishers, Halley Court, Jordan Hill, Oxford, OX2 8EJ.

MADRID ATHENS PARIS FLORENCE PORTSMOUTH NH CHICAGO
SAO PAULO SINGAPORE TOKYO MELBOURNE AUCKLAND
IBADAN GABORONE JOHANNESBURG KAMPALA NAIROBI

British Library Cataloguing in Publication Data
A catalogue record for this book is available from the British Library.

ISBN 0 431 01613 5 (hardback) 0 431 01618 6 (paperback)

PLEASE READ THIS
**For some of the activities in this book, you will need to use
tools and materials, such as scissors or a knife, plant material
and soil. Be very careful when you are using them, and always
make sure an adult is there to help you.**
* Don't sniff mouldy materials, or put them in your mouth.
* If your skin is unusually sensitive, don't handle plant material.
* Always wash your hands after doing any of these activities!

Edited by Valerie Wyatt and Alex Gray
Designed by James Ireland
Printed in Hong Kong

Table of contents

Is it alive?

Living things are all around you. They can be plants, animals, fungi or tiny bacteria, but they all have some characteristics in common:

• Living things are made of cells. Cells are the building blocks of life. The cells in your body make up the organs that help you see, breathe, grow, move and do many other things.

• Living things need food, air, water and a habitat (a place to live).

• Living things grow, reproduce (breed) and respond to the environment around them.

There are seven living things on this page. Can you find them?

Worm farm

All living things need food to live and grow. Why not make a worm farm and watch what happens when some worms start eating?

You will need:
- garden soil or potting compost
- a large, wide-mouthed jar
- a water spray
- sand
- apple and carrot peelings
- 4 earthworms (look for them on the path or in a garden after it rains)
- black sugar paper and tape

What to do:
1. Put a layer of soil 2.5 cm deep in the bottom of the jar. Use the spray to moisten the soil. Add a 2.5-cm layer of sand. Repeat layers until you are 5 cm from the top of the jar. Fill the rest of the jar with peelings.

2. Put the worms on top of the peelings.

3. Tape the sugar paper around the outside of the jar and put the jar in a dark place. Now wash your hands! Don't disturb the jar for a week, except to add more peelings and a sprinkling of water once during the week.

4. After a week, carefully remove the sugar paper. Can you see the worm trails? When you have finished observing your worm farm, empty it into the soil outside.

What's happening?
Earthworms are part of nature's way of fertilizing the soil. The peelings and other food they eat are broken down as they pass through their digestive system. Then the bits of food are deposited in the soil as 'casts'. The casts help to enrich the soil so that plants will grow better.

Living things need food
All living things need food to give them energy for growth and repair. Living things get food in different ways. Animals must find plants or other animals to eat. Plants make their own food (see page 8).

Tattoo a plant

Plants can't eat, so they need to make their own food. How do plants do this? Grow a plant and find out.

You will need:

- scissors
- cardboard
- 3 paper clips
- a young pot plant, stood in a dish so you can water it.

What to do:

1. Ask an adult to cut the first letter of your name, or any other shape, out of the cardboard. This is your tattoo. Cut out three tattoos.

2. Use a paper clip to attach the cardboard tattoos to the upper surface of the leaves of the plant — put one tattoo on each leaf.

3. Put the plant in a sunny spot (but not too hot). Water it to keep the soil moist but not too wet.

4. After a week, remove the tattoos. What do the leaves look like? Wait another week. How do the leaves look?

What's happening?

The cells in a plant's leaves are like tiny factories. They make food using light, water, a gas called carbon dioxide, and chlorophyll, a chemical that makes leaves green. This process is called photosynthesis. When you covered part of a leaf with the tattoo, light couldn't reach the cells in that part of the leaf, so food stopped being made there. What do you think would happen if you covered the whole leaf?

Feed a fungus

To make bread, you need a living thing — a fungus called yeast. Like all living things, yeast needs to eat. But what?

You will need:
- 3 small drinking glasses, each with 125 ml (½ cup) warm water
- 15 ml (1 tablespoon) sugar
- 15 ml (1 tablespoon) salt
- 45 ml (3 tablespoons) baking yeast

What to do:
1. Stir the sugar into one glass of water and the salt into another.
2. Sprinkle 15 ml (1 tablespoon) yeast into each of the three glasses and stir.
3. Put the glasses in a warm place and watch them for 5 minutes. Which glass has the most foamy bubbles?

What's happening?
When yeast likes food, it produces bubbles of carbon dioxide gas. The more it likes the food, the more bubbles it makes. Which food did your yeast prefer? When bread is baked, the bubbles burst and leave holes.

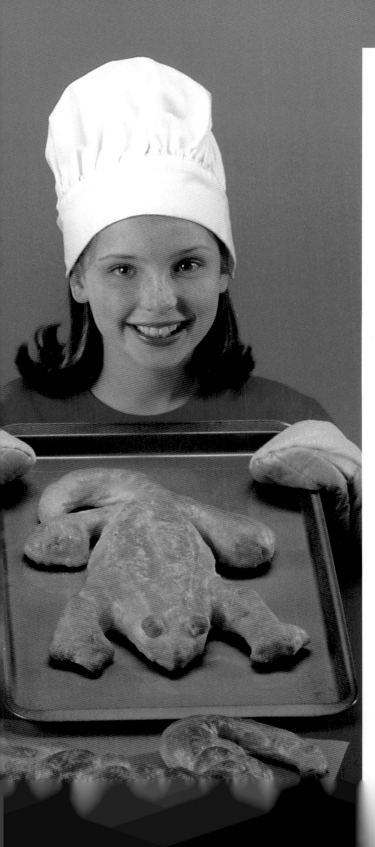

BAKE BREAD
Use yeast to bake some bread.

You will need:
- 500 ml (2 cups) very warm water
- 15 ml (1 tablespoon) each of sugar, yeast, vegetable oil and salt
- 1.25 litres (5 cups) white flour
- baking sheet, lightly oiled

What to do:
1. Pour the warm water into a bowl. Stir in the sugar then sprinkle the yeast on top. Put the bowl in a warm place for 10 minutes. The yeast should bubble.
2. Stir in the oil and salt and slowly add the flour. Use your hands, if you wish.
3. On a floured surface, punch and fold the dough for 10 minutes — until it's smooth. Add more flour if it's too sticky.
4. Put the dough into a clean, oiled bowl. Cover with a clean tea towel and place somewhere warm until the dough has doubled in size — for about 2 hours.
5. Roll the dough out on a floured surface until it is 2.5 cm thick. Make the dough into any shape you wish.
6. Ask an adult to put your dough on a baking sheet in an oven heated to 120°C 350°F, Gas Mark 4, for about 30 minutes.

How's your breathing?

Breathe in. Now breathe out. You need air to live and grow. Other living things need air, too. How much air do you need? Here's how to find out.

You will need:
- a 4-litre plastic milk jug
- a piece of plastic tubing 0.5 m long (available at hardware shops)
- a measuring cup

What to do:
1. Fill the milk jug full of water.
2. Half fill a sink or large bowl with water.
3. Cover the opening of the jug with your hand. Turn the jug upside down and put the opening down into the water. Remove your hand.
4. Ask a friend to hold the jug. Put one end of the tubing into the jug.
5. Breathe in, then blow into the tubing. Blow out as much air as you can.

6. Remove the tubing. Cover the opening of the jug with your hand. Lift the jug out of the water and turn it the right way up.
7. Use the measuring cup to fill up the jug. How much water did you add? This is how much air you breathed out.

What's happening?
When you blow air into the jug, an equal volume of water has to leave the jug. This is like breathing. When you breathe in fresh air, you have to breathe out an equal amount of used air.

Why do we breathe?
When animals breathe, they exchange new air for used air. This brings oxygen to the blood. The body needs oxygen to operate properly. Breathing out gets rid of carbon dioxide, a waste gas that is no longer needed. Even plants 'breathe'. Carbon dioxide and oxygen move in and out through tiny openings in their leaves.

Egg heads

You are full of water — it is in your blood, in your cells, even in your bones. All living things need water. But how much? Grow some cress to find out.

You will need:
- a small nail
- 3 eggs
- a bowl
- 3 cotton balls
- some cress seeds

What to do:
1. Using the nail, carefully make a hole about the size of a penny in one end of each egg.
2. Hold the eggs over the bowl and let the insides drain out. Rinse any remaining raw egg out of the eggshells. (You can use the insides for cooking.)
3. Put a cotton ball into each egg shell.
4. Sprinkle enough seeds on each cotton ball to cover it.
5. Add just enough water to one egg shell to moisten the cotton ball thoroughly. Fill the second egg shell with water so that the cotton and seeds are completely covered. Do not water the third egg shell.
6. Put the egg shells in a sunny place. Over the next week, keep the cotton ball in the first one moist, and the seeds in the second one covered with water. Which egg head do you think will grow the best cress 'hair'?

What's happening?
Like all living things, seeds need water to grow. The outer coating on the seed softens, and the roots, stems and leaves begin to grow from it. But seeds can have too much water. In the egg with the most water, the seeds couldn't get any air, so they didn't grow. In the picture on the right, which egg head do you think got just the right amount of water?

Living things need water

The cells that living things are made of need just the right amount of water to work properly. Without water, living things will die.

Bottle habitat

Imagine you had to live in the ocean. Would you need special equipment? Water is not our natural home. Humans live on land, surrounded by air. All living things have a habitat, a place where they prefer to live. What kind of habitat does a wood louse prefer?

You will need:

- a 2-litre plastic drinks bottle with cap
- scissors
- damp soil
- some large leaves
- 6 live wood lice

You can find wood lice under large stones or logs.

What to do:

1. Ask an adult to cut a flap in the bottle as shown.
2. Add damp soil to the bottle until it is half full.

3. Put the leaves on top of the soil at one end of the bottle.

4. Add the wood lice to the bottle. Close the flap and lay the drinks bottle on its side in a bright place.

5. Wait 20 minutes, then count the wood lice at each end of the bottle.

What's happening?

Did most wood lice like the end with the leaves or the end without? They probably chose the leafy end, because it is dark and shady like their usual habitat. Now that you know what your wood lice prefer, turn the whole bottle into a wood louse habitat. When you are finished observing your wood lice, empty the bottle outside.

Living things need a habitat

Different kinds of living things prefer different habitats. For example, fish live in water, and earthworms live in the soil. Some plants prefer the sun, others grow well in the shade. The world is full of different habitats.

The eating game

Take a look at yourself in a mirror. Do you have the same kind of mouth as a frog or bird? Why not? Try this game with some friends and find out.

You will need:
- a handful each of rice, elastic bands, marbles, cereal, dried pasta, sweets
- some kitchen tools such as a clothes peg, spoon, toothpick, plastic fork and tongs
- a small plastic bag for each player
- a watch with a second hand

What to do:
1. Give each player a clothes peg, spoon, tongs, toothpick or other tool. These are your 'mouths'.
2. Put the rice, elastic bands, marbles and other objects in separate piles on a table. This is your 'food'.
3. Give one plastic bag to each player. This is your 'stomach'.

4. The object of the gme is to use your 'mouth' to put as much 'food' as possible into your 'stomach'. Each player gets 30 seconds to collect food.

What's happening?
Do some 'mouths' work better for certain foods than others? Animals have different mouths because they eat different foods. A frog needs a fast-moving, sticky tongue to snatch insects out of the air. A hummingbird uses its beak like a straw to sip nectar from flowers. You have strong teeth and jaws to bite and chew plants and meat.

Living things are adapted to their environment
Plant and animal bodies are adapted to the foods they eat and places they live. Look at birds' feet, for example. Why do you think some birds have claws while others have webbed feet? Plants are adapted, too. For example, desert plants like cacti can store water to survive long, dry spells.

Dirt dwellers

Who lives in the soil? Make this creature-catcher and find out.

You will need:

- a large, wide-mouthed jar
- a funnel
- a small piece of screen (cut from a plastic pot scourer)
- soil from a garden
- a lamp
- paper towel
- a magnifying glass (if you have one)

What to do:

1. Set the funnel in the mouth of the jar and cover the opening to the narrow neck of the funnel with the screen.

2. Fill the funnel with soil.

3. From at least 20 cm, shine the light onto the soil. Turn out all the other lights and leave the lamp on overnight.

4. In the morning, remove the funnel and empty the jar onto a paper towel. Look at the creatures — use a magnifying glass, if you have one. Are all the creatures the same?

What's happening?

Most soil animals prefer moist, dark places. They burrow down through the soil to escape the heat and light of the lamp and fall into the jar. Return the animals to the soil in your garden when you have finished.

There is variety in living things

How many different types of creatures did you find? Living things come in many shapes, sizes and colours. Variety is important in nature. For example, what if all living things ate the same food? Would there be enough food to go around?

Fingerprint detective

Here's a mystery. What do you have that no-one else has? Become a detective and find out.

You will need:
- a soft (2B) lead pencil
- scrap paper
- transparent sticky tape
- white paper
- a magnifying glass

What to do:
1. Scribble on the scrap paper to make a very dark area of pencil lead.
2. Rub your first finger in the lead.
3. Stick a small piece of tape across the pencil smudge on your finger, then gently peel off the tape. Your fingerprint will come off with it.
4. Stick the tape to a piece of white paper. Repeat with your other fingers, then wash your hands.
5. Take a close look at your fingerprints with a magnifying glass.
6. Compare them with fingerprints from your friends and family.

What's happening?
Nobody else has fingerprints exactly like yours — not even if you are an identical twin. There are always slight differences in living things. Some of these differences can be important. For example, a bird of prey with sharp eyesight has a better chance of finding food than one with weak eyesight.

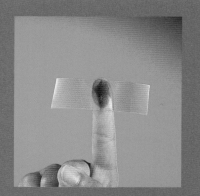

Life cycles

You grow bigger as you grow older, but some living things seem to change their bodies completely during their life. This is called 'metamorphosis'. Try raising some mealworms and watch them go through a complete change. This activity may take up to six weeks.

You will need:
- a clear container with a lid
- bran and potato or apple wedges
- 6 mealworms (available at pet shops)
- paper towel

What to do:
1. Almost fill the container with bran. Set potato or apple wedges on top, sprinkle on the mealworms. Put the lid on and put the container in a shed.
2. Check the mealworms every few days and replace the apple or potato wedges if they dry up or go mouldy. Also add more bran if necessary. Always replace the lid!

3. Twice a week, gently sprinkle the bran out onto a paper towel and take a look to see what changes have taken place. Can you find the three stages of the mealworm's metamorphosis shown on page 25? (The fourth stage — the egg — is too small to see.)

What's happening?
A mealworm goes through four stages of change in its life cycle. It changes from a **larva** (worm) to a **pupa** to an adult **beetle**, which lays the **eggs** that hatch into new larvae. Birth, growth, reproduction and death make up the life cycle of living things.

Metamorphosis
Some other animals, including frogs and butterflies, go through metamorphosis, too. Why do they change their shape? Having two forms means they can eat different foods and live in different habitats at different times during their life cycle. So they do not depend on just one food or habitat.

larva (worm) stage

pupa stage

adult beetle stage

Flower power

Flowers come in all shapes and sizes. Here's how to make a simple flower press and start a flower collection.

You will need:

- a hole punch
- 2 pieces of cardboard 15 cm x 15 cm square
- 2 shoelaces
- flowers (use flowers from your garden or a shop, not wild flowers)
- paper towels
- a heavy book

What to do:

1. Punch holes in the corners of both pieces of cardboard.
2. Lace the shoelaces through the holes as shown.

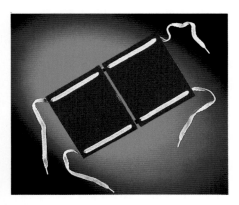

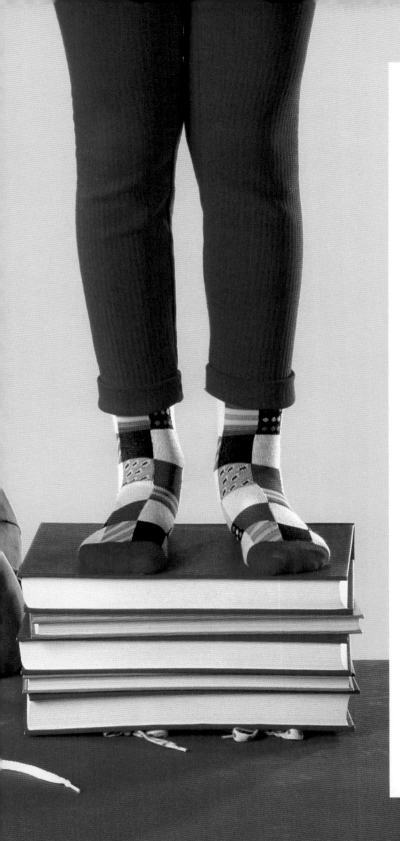

3. Place your flowers between two paper towels and put them into your plant press.

4. Tightly tie the edges of your press together and put the press under the heavy book.

5. After four days, carefully remove the pressed flowers and display your collection. How many different shapes and colours of flowers did you find?

Flowers and insects

Pretty shapes and colours are two ways flowers attract insects. Scent is another. Why do flowers need to attract insects? Insects carry pollen from the male part of the flower in one plant to the female part in another plant so that seeds can form and grow into new plants.

Living things reproduce

All living things die eventually. To keep their species alive, they must create new living things. Plants produce seeds, chickens lay eggs, dogs have puppies, and your parents had you. This is called reproduction.

Secret smells

How do you communicate, or send messages? With your voice? Your eyes? Or do you use body language, such as hand gestures ? How about with smell? Many plants — and even some animals — use smell to communicate. Can you pick up a scent signal?

You will need:
- cotton balls
- vanilla extract
- 5 empty film canisters (or other small containers)
- a blindfold

What to do:
1. Soak the cotton balls in vanilla extract and place some in each film canister.
2. In a safe place in your home or garden, set out a scent trail for a friend. Put the film canisters, with the cotton balls, about 1 m apart to make a trail.
3. Blindfold your friend and see if they can follow the trail just by sniffing.
4. Change places. Get your friend to set the scent trail, and you try to follow it.

Living things communicate
Many insects, such as ants, communicate with one another using scent trails. Other living things use colours and patterns, sounds or body language. These signals may be used to warn of danger or show anger or help to attract a mate.

For parents and teachers

The activities in this book are designed to teach children about the characteristics and basic needs of living things. Some experiments explore living things' requirements for food, air, water and a habitat. Other activities introduce the concepts of growth, reproduction, adaptation and communication. Here are some ideas to extend the activities in this book.

Is it alive?

Look around you for objects that have been made from living things. Many everyday items are made from materials that were once alive, such as paper, wood, wool, cotton, silk, and cork.

Worm farm

Bacteria and fungi also decompose, or rot, the peelings returning nutrients to the soil. To see what bacteria and fungi do, set up a worm farm minus the worms. After a week, examine the peelings without opening the jar.

Tattoo a plant

To see the other pigments, besides green, in leaves, tear some leaves into small pieces, place them in a jar and cover with rubbing alcohol. After five minutes dip one end of a strip of coffee filter paper into the solution. When the strip is completely wet, remove it and let it dry.

Feed a fungus

Mould is another type of fungus. To observe moulds, leave slices of different foods on a kitchen counter for an hour, then place them in separate airtight plastic bags and seal them. Put the bags in a dark cupboard and observe every few days. Do not open the bags.

How's your breathing?

Plants take in gases to help make food during photosynthesis and release waste gases back into the air. The gases pass through openings called stoma on the leaves. Cover the underside of one plant leaf with petroleum jelly and watch what happens over several days.

Egg heads

How much water do living things contain? Cut slices of different fruits and vegetables. The longer they take to dry, the more water they contain.

Pop-bottle habitat

Plants have habitats, too. Look for different plants in shady, sunny, wet and dry habitats in a garden or park.

The eating game

Observe birds in the wild or a zoo or in pictures, and compare their beaks to kitchen utensils and other tools.

Dirt dwellers

A suitable school project would be to gather dirt samples from a variety of habitats. Compare the variety of animals found in the different habitats.

Fingerprint detective

Look for other traits that are controlled genetically. See who can roll their tongue, spread their toes, wiggle their small toe sideways, or flare their nostrils. Can all of the members of a family do the same things?

Life cycles

There are many other examples of metamorphosis. Parents and teachers could show children that caterpillars change into a pupa and then an adult moth or butterfly, dragonfly larvae into dragonflies, or tadpoles change into frogs

Flower power and Secret smells

In a garden, follow an insect. Which flowers does it prefer? Do certain insects prefer particular colours, shapes or smells?

Animals sometimes use body language to communicate. Try using your body to say: danger!, come here, stay away, and other messages.

Words to know

bacteria: simple, one-celled organisms that can break down (rot) animal or vegetable material

chlorophyll: the chemical in plants that makes leaves green. It is needed for photosynthesis.

digestive system: the parts of an animal's body where food is broken down and passed on to other parts of the body

fungi: a group of living things that are neither plants nor animals. Mould, mushrooms and yeast are types of fungi.

metamorphosis: a process that some animals undergo as they grow into an adult. It involves several changes to their body form.

mould: a kind of fungus that grows on food, rotting plants and dead animals

photosynthesis: the process by which green plants make their own food, using carbon dioxide (a gas in the air), sunlight and water

reproduction: the process by which living things create new life

seeds: tiny baby plants protected by a covering

Index